The Summer Without a Motorcycle

A Spiritual Realization of Freedom from the Stresses of Modern Life

By: Doug Milbrand

Copyright © Douglas E. Milbrand, 2011
All rights reserved

Cover Design by: Jimmy Campbell
Philadelphia, PA
www.arthead.us

Soft Cover ISBN: 978-0-9833956-0-7

Printed in the United States of America

Printed By: Morgantown Printing and Binding
Morgantown, WV

Except in the United States of America, this book is sold subject to the condition that it shall not, by the way of trade or otherwise, be lent, resold, hired out, or otherwise circulated without the publisher's prior consent in any form of binding or cover other than that in which it is published and without a similar condition including this condition being imposed on the subsequent purchaser.

The scanning, uploading and distribution of this book via the Internet or via any other means without the permission of the publisher is illegal and punishable by law. Please purchase only authorized electronic editions, and do not participate in or encourage electronic piracy of copyrighted materials. Your support of the author's rights is appreciated.

Acknowledgements

I am eternally grateful for my great family and friends, and the good fortune in my life. Each one of you has played an integral part in making me who I am today, and I thank you for it.

To my wife, Amy: Without you and your constant reassurance and support, I would not be half the man I am today. You have made my life complete. You are my best friend and partner in life and I look forward to living out the rest of our dreams together.

I would especially like to thank my parents, Jim and Sharon. You have always shown Greg, Gary and me unconditional love and taught us gratefulness, patience and perseverance. You instilled in us a never quit attitude, even in trying times, and assured us we would make it through.

Contents

I. The Self-Evaluation 3

II. The Expenses 15

III. The Awakening 29

IV. The Future 46

I used to earn a paycheck and pay for "things" first, then live on whatever was left. Now, I earn a paycheck to live first and buy "things" with what is left.

The Summer Without a Motorcycle

I. The Self-Evaluation

It was the spring and about half way through Amy's and my new journey when a friend of ours, Alyssa, asked me to help her with a college psychology paper to relate the theories she was learning in class to my personality traits. Since I had never taken a psychology class in college, I found this experience to be quite interesting.

The report attempted to show how the conscious, unconscious and external factors throughout my life evolved and developed my thoughts and actions over the course of many years. It explained how these factors affected and influenced my behaviors and relationships with others, and helped me to overcome the challenges I faced throughout life. In order to better understand the behavioral traits as they related to the theories discussed in her class, we first discussed my upbringing.

I was born a middle child with two brothers in a middle class family. Alyssa explained Alfred Adler's birth order theory to me and we discussed how that might have impacted my behavior throughout life. Adler theorized that the middle child is more independent and competitive and struggles to identify their role in the family. The second child can adopt a negative trait and become rebellious, especially if they do not feel they are getting equal treatment. A second child can also adapt and acquire positive traits such as great social skills and creativity, and tend to be more expressive. I immediately related to these descriptions and my mind began racing with memories.

My dad was a music teacher and band director; so other than family vacations, I hardly remember a time when I did not have at least fifty other "siblings" along for the trip. It gave me the opportunity to see parts of the country I might not have otherwise seen, but with two brothers, plus an additional "extended family" around me most of the time, I had to define myself early in life in order to stand out in the crowd and be noticed. Being the middle child built my character into a strong-willed, but sometimes stubborn person.

Since I can remember, I have always been rebellious and was sent to the principal's office more often than my parents and any other parent would have liked. For example, my elementary school had a narrow, tiled hallway leading into the bathroom. I do not recall whose idea it was, but a few friends and I got caught climbing up between the walls as if to be superheroes. Not only did this get the attention of my parents, it also involved attention from many other teachers, students and the principal.

Most of the time, I was the first of the siblings to try daring stunts such as homemade bicycle jumps, go-carts and dismounting the swing at its highest point. Because of this, I was the one most likely to end up in the emergency room or at least requiring bandages and gauze. Greg, Gary and our neighbors across the street, Jason and Dan, definitely influenced my decisions by daring me to attempt such stunts.

Alyssa explained to me that, because I risked injury, the bicycle stunts could be considered a negative influence. However, my brothers and friends created desires to exceed and be recognized which could be considered a positive influence for developing my character.

Alyssa and I then discussed the Freudian perspective, and the impact this had on shaping my personality. By having the desire to stand out among siblings and peers, I let what Freud calls my "id" control most of my actions beyond the infant stages into toddler and through adolescence. Rosamund and Benjamin Zander describe this in the book *The Art of Possibility* as the calculating self; a coping mechanism to receive attention and "fit in" with the crowd. For the most part, negative reinforcement did not work with me since, even though I was in trouble, I still got the desired result of attention from my parents and others. Even though I knew that getting into things I should not have, like climbing the bathroom walls, would be frowned upon, I did not care about the consequences and I continued this pattern of misbehavior. Acting out through stubbornness to control people and circumstances around me became a part of my personality.

As I grew through adolescence and young adulthood, these ambitions continued as I unknowingly attempted to match or surpass my peers in jobs, material possessions and activities. This desire to succeed pushed me to attend college for a degree in electrical engineering. After all, my older brother Greg was already in college taking courses such as molecular biology.

Raised as a Catholic, I heard all the teachings in church and Sunday school, but never really had a spiritual awakening until college. I quickly realized that my childish ways did not work in the "real world" and I could not have everything I wanted, when I wanted it, through stubbornness and manipulation. It was at this time I realized the morals and values my family and the church taught me would first be put to the test.

I knew the Holy Spirit instilled in me to become, as international Catholic speaker and author Matthew Kelly defines it, "the best version of myself." With the constant temptation of alcohol, sex and drugs so often found in college, I found myself relying on my upbringing to guide my decision-making and stay the course to obtain my degree. Do not misunderstand me, I like a good party, but I had to control myself so as not to go overboard and lose my focus on why I was there. I had to make compromises in order to satisfy my life instinct for survival.

I recall my sophomore year of college as being the most difficult for me. I had completed my general studies courses and was getting into the core classes of engineering, which proved difficult to juggle with a social life and activities such as the college marching band. My grade point average was suffering because I had contracted mononucleosis the previous year, and consequently missed two weeks of class at the beginning of my college career.

My parents always taught us to never give up, even in trying times. I distinctly remember calling home and talking to my dad, wanting to give up and move back home. Minus the illness, my dad had apparently been through the same thing in college and could relate to my situation. He talked me through it, my stubbornness prevailed and I continued on with college.

My sophomore year was also the same year I began to let my faith start taking control of my life, especially when I felt overwhelmed. Throughout these times, I had continued to attend church, praying that the Lord would take care of me and see me through the tough times. I remember the homilies from Father Bill about putting your stress, anxiety and worry in the Lord's hands and to let his plan work.

Matthew 11:28-30 tells us,

> *"Come to me and I will give you rest – all of you who work so hard beneath a heavy yoke. Wear my yoke – for it fits perfectly – and let me teach you; for I am gentle and humble, and you shall find rest for*

your souls; for I give you only light burdens."

In other words, the Lord will not give you more than you can handle in life.

That same year I met a wonderful local family that welcomed me into their family. I attended church with them fairly regularly and even got a "job" tutoring math to the youngest daughter in exchange for a free dinner that was not from the dormitory cafeteria. Between the hour or so of peace in church and their hospitality, it was a nice break once a week to escape my life as an engineering student.

My final, what some may call "super-senior" year of college, I met Amy. After we started dating, I knew we were going to be together for a long time, possibly forever. But she still had three years of college to finish; so unless I found a job locally we would have a long distance relationship. I knew we would get through it if it was meant to be, and we have been together ever since.

The summer after graduating from college, I moved back into my parents' house to begin my career search while maintaining a long distance relationship with Amy. I would wake up every morning, browse the jobs posted on the Internet and apply for those that matched the type of career I was seeking. By that time, it was nice enough outside to lie in the pool for a few hours. After that I would go to the gym with Gary and Dan for a workout. For spending money, I worked odds and ends jobs such as moving furniture and mowing lawns. I must admit, it was a nice summer, but I knew it could not last forever. Toward the end of that summer, I landed an engineering career.

With my job security taking care of my physiological needs, a steady girlfriend who I knew I would one day marry, and a loving family behind me, my self-esteem was the highest I had ever known.

II. The Expenses

I speak from experience in saying that teachers do not get paid nearly enough salary for forming the future of America on a daily basis. My dad worked tirelessly year-round for the benefit of others' children. Even with my dad teaching, my mom worked various jobs in addition to supporting him at his extra-curricular events. This was just to make enough money to feed themselves and three growing boys. I remember my mom used to come home from the grocery store, unpack the food and it would, for the most part, be gone the next day. And that was without any friends coming over to visit.

We did not have extra money to spare while growing up, but my parents always taught us that God provided enough for us to get by, and he did. We never had the latest Air Jordans, but at least we had Zips shoes on our feet. However, since we did not have extra money lying around, I never knew how to interact with it very well. My brothers and I were raised with a reward system for achievement. If we received good grades and made the honor role, for example, we were rewarded with a desired item from a store, such as a new cassette tape or action figure.

Throughout high school, my brothers and I worked during the summers, but the only bill we had to pay was for our car insurance premiums in order to get to and from work and around town. If I recall correctly, we spent the rest of our earnings mostly on electronics. I never related hard work to saving and giving money, only spending and receiving.

At the same time, growing up in this American culture I have been bombarded with commercials that told me to buy this item, wear this brand of clothing and drink this particular sugar. If I did, it would make me feel better or be accepted. Society had implanted these ideals in my mind, and I did not repress them as much as I should have.

When I got to college, I worked during the summer to pay for car insurance, but also to save money for books. I took out student loans for tuition. I did fairly well in college with spending money, but my "spending" money was provided by my parents, not through working. As I mentioned, I ate at the dormitory cafeteria even beyond my freshman year when I lived off campus. For extra spending money on the weekend, I would call my parents every so often and ask for $30 to do laundry. I would do my laundry but only the clothes that fit into two washers and dryers would get washed. Total cost: about $10. I would then have the other $20 for nights on the town and the occasional fast food indulgence.

Upon graduating from college and getting a job as an engineer, I was on the market for a vehicle. In constant search of self-actualization and exceeding the standards set by society and my siblings, I bought a brand new car, even prior to getting my first paycheck. This car was loaded with all the bells and whistles, power everything and leather interior. As when I was a child, I felt I had control of my life once again and instead of considering the consequences of a car payment for five years, I got what I wanted, and it felt good at the time. This is what I learned Freud calls "the pleasure principle" in action. Although I did not realize it at the time, I had reverted back to my childish ways.

I justified the purchase in every way possible. I "needed" a safe, reliable means of transportation to go visit my long-distance girlfriend four and a half hours away on the weekends. A brand new car would not leave me stranded, right? That was another justification I used. A year into the payments, I had an issue with the power control module and the car was in the service shop for nearly a week. Sure, it was covered under warranty, but it was definitely an inconvenience. In addition to safe and reliable transportation, I also needed to build my credit score because that is what society told me I had to do in order to survive and win financially.

Shortly after I saved a little bit of money, I bought a motorcycle from my dad because I had been riding every summer since I was seventeen years old and should not have to go without one for too long.

About a year later, I moved in with a roommate to rent a house with acreage. It was then I realized I needed a truck as well. Since there was no service to the house, I had to take the garbage to the dump. I bought a used two-wheel drive truck in addition to the car and financed it through the bank. So now, I am paying car, truck and student loan payments in addition to the rent.

The following year I got engaged to Amy and the wedding was planned for a year later. Because it was close to a median distance between our parents, we decided on settling down, at least temporarily, in the Allegheny Mountains of Pennsylvania. I heard they received considerable amounts of snow, so I would need a four-wheel drive vehicle; and I did not have one. In addition, everyone had told me "I had to get my toys before we got married or I would never get them." So I sold the old truck and the car, received some money out of them and used it for a down payment on a brand new four-wheel drive truck a couple months prior to the wedding. I felt this was great. I was realizing the equity in the vehicles and also building my credit score since I knew a house purchase would be in the near future.

Amy and I got married and decided to rent a townhouse for a year until we got a better feel for the area. She got a job at the local television station with her marketing degree and therefore needed a safe, reliable car to get to and from work. We went shopping for a new mattress for our townhouse and in addition to the mattress, ended up driving a gently used car home for her. A few months later, she ended up not liking the high-pressure sales job and left the company. Luckily, within a short time, she picked up another job at a local jewelry store, but the payments remained.

Just a year later, we bought a house with no money down and Private Mortgage Insurance, or PMI. We now thought we were living the American dream. Up to this point, I was never upside down on a vehicle, meaning I did not owe more than the vehicle was worth, and did not miss any payments. Our credit scores were through the roof, we had dependable vehicles, a motorcycle for cruising and a house we could call our own. We were winning at our new life together, right? By society's standards, I would have to say yes.

Looking back, my biggest downward turning point is when I turned to vanity for self-actualization. Shortly after we moved into the house, I sold the old motorcycle and bought my dream bike, a Harley Davidson. We were capable of making the payments, so I had to have it. I called Amy on the way to look at the bike. She said, "We don't have money for a Harley Davidson" to which I replied, "The bank says we do." I bought it a few days later. Although we enjoyed it and would take long rides together, it was not the dream I had always imagined it to be. The following summer we rode it from Pennsylvania to South Carolina. We soon found out that for trips longer than about two hours, the unbalanced "EVO" motor was a rough ride and would put our limbs to sleep.

Amy took a job at my engineering company, which doubled her income over the jewelry store, so we decided to trade her car in for a gently used luxury SAV. This way, if kids came along in the near future, we would have an SAV that was already paid down, or paid off. We thought; it does not get any more reliable or safe than this SAV. I do not know if we bought a lemon or the Lord was trying to tell us something, but that vehicle broke down every other month for the short duration we owned it.

One particularly frustrating incident occurred while driving from the airport after a week-long cruise. We were returning to our hometown when one of the pulleys stopped and left us stranded along the highway in the middle of the night. We had to unload all our luggage, get a tow truck to take us to the nearest gas station where we could wait for my parents to pick us up and take us back to their house. The next morning we were able to call a vehicle rental agency so we could make it the rest of the way home.

Luckily the SAV was a certified pre-owned, so the repairs did not cost anything but a small deductible, but it was once again a hassle. What made the situation even worse was that for the first time we had rolled over negative equity from the car and we were upside down on the value. So I reverted back to what I had known and done before and thought was smart. I sold my four-wheel drive truck to realize the equity in it and pay down the SAV to the breakeven point.

Instead of learning from that experience, I continued to stubbornly swap out vehicles every two years rolling the equity from one into the other, trying to get ahead that way.

Once I had a little bit of equity in my older motorcycle, I traded it for a brand new pearl white Harley Davidson. Now this was my dream bike! Between the production years of my old bike and that of this new bike, they had fixed every issue I had ever complained about, including the engine vibration. Amy also loved this bike and was included in the purchase decision this time.

Between the two of us, we owned, sold or traded twelve vehicles throughout eleven years. So here we were with payments on a mortgage, car, truck, motorcycle, student loan, home equity loan, and a revolving credit card that we paid off every month. I also had intentions for renovations of a project truck that would require spare money to finish. Does this not sound like the typical American household?

I must admit we were struggling in our marriage at this point in time. Amy always told me we should have a few months savings put away for an emergency. I would always ask her how, with all these bills, are we supposed to save money? Our communication broke down because I was too stubborn to try something different because, after all, we were winning. All the while, something kept reminding me that this was an inappropriate way to live. I often wondered if this was what life was about and as good as it gets. I have a successful career, a great wife, and the toy I had always dreamed of, but something was still amiss.

I also felt bad because I had convinced my brother he could afford a motorcycle through my rationalizations of net worth. With life insurance, as long as he had a positive net worth, if anything were to happen to him, he would not leave a burden to anyone. After all, that was the way I had been living for years.

Through my faith and my upbringing, I always had the good feeling of a giving heart and liked helping people; yet I was barely able to give $20 when the offering came around on Sunday. I felt like I was living the story of Zacchaeus, taking more than my fair share in this world, and I needed a different view on life.

As I have done throughout my life I continued to pray for guidance. I constantly thought to myself that there had to be something more to my life than just going to work to buy things and living month-to-month.

III. The Awakening

I have never been much into politics throughout my life and always thought the Government is going to do what it is going to do and, other than voting between the lesser of two evils in an election, I was not able to do anything about it. As did most Americans, in the most recent Presidential election, I began to grow more concerned about the growing national debt. Even though Amy and I do not yet have children, we plan to someday. I want to leave this country and this world a better place than before, and do not want to leave a debt for the generations to come.

During my master's degree studies, I learned of Maslow's hierarchy of needs which theorizes that people prioritize fundamental needs before realizing their full potential. It seems to me as though people in this country have become self-absorbed, putting their self-actualization ahead of basic needs and security; therefore, they have to rely on the Government for these basic needs. People are running around trying to outdo the next person with lifestyle and the Government is encouraging it.

Take the "cash-for-clunkers" program for example. Through the tax-funded program, Americans were offered $4,000 in trade for a vehicle worth $2,000; but only if they traded on a new vehicle, thereby making most people go further into debt with payments. This was in total disagreement with my intent of leaving the world a better place for the next generation, and I was being forced by a government to participate in it. If the Government would stop taking twenty to thirty percent of pay every year for these types of material possession programs, the American people would have more to give to hospitals, churches and research for the betterment of humanity.

The more I thought about it, the more I realized that by borrowing I was part of the problem. I always thought that as long as our net worth was positive and we were not behind on our bills we were not living beyond our means. But by carrying around our debt, we were contributing to the burden on future society. As I have always done in the past, I started to pray about it that I may be able to fix myself and our marriage so as not to be a negative contributor to the world.

One day, I do not recall the exact moment, but my eyes were opened and my life was about to be transformed. God had been speaking to me for quite some time, but I had just not taken the time to listen. If you recall the verse from Matthew 11, the Lord had not given me more than I could handle. Instead, I had piled myself and our relationship with the heavy yoke and we both had to work hard just to keep up with life.

Looking back, there were several incidents that happened over the previous year that were cues about which direction to head in life. One turning point was when I told my mom I got a raise at work and what my annual income now was. She asked, "What do you do with all your money?" It caught me off guard and I did not have a good answer. I knew it was all going to payments for "things" and felt somewhat ashamed. That made me realize I needed to change.

Also in the previous year, I had been asked to be a Godfather to my niece, Kayla and a good friend's son, Garrett. I began to wonder how I could do God's will with my life if I was too involved fulfilling my own will. How was I to teach these children to live more Christ-like when I myself was not doing a very good job of it?

But how was I to change my way of life, especially when dealing with our spending and finances? One last incident came in a car ride with coworkers and friends Dan and Mike. During a business trip, knowing I was a Christian, they listened to what I thought at the time was this weird guy named Dave Ramsey for four and a half hours. I argued the entire trip, nitpicking all the technical details. We paid off the credit card every month and received the rewards points. Our credit scores were great, and we were rolling equity over from vehicle-to-vehicle and getting ahead by paying them down.

However, the economy was becoming worse and I still had this weighted down feeling that if something such as a layoff or medical emergency ever happened, we would not be able to make all these monthly payments. We were living life on the edge. At the same time, Amy continued to remind me that we needed some savings in case of this type of emergency. I also started to take a better look at an early retirement so that I was not working the rest of my life.

I decided to stop being stubborn and try something new. Since I was still a bit skeptical of anyone telling me how to build wealth and there was not a class offered within forty-five miles of where we lived, we bought the *Dave Ramsey's Financial Peace University* DVD set from a church off of the Internet. We watched the series over the next couple of months at our own pace.

Amy and I sat down together with our finances and put everything out on the table. We aligned our values and goals and began communicating again. We once again became excited about our future.

When we learned about eliminating debt, I knew the first step in the process was not going to be easy. Since I had the motorcycle of my dreams, but it still had payments, it was the first debt we were able to eliminate. After some heartbreak, we sold it within a few weeks of starting the class. We then rolled the equity we had in it, plus the monthly payments into Amy's car. Within a month of starting the classes, it was paid off.

The key to staying out of debt during this process is to have some money in savings, so in case of an emergency, we would not have to go back into debt. This was put to the test almost immediately. A week after we got the car paid off, we were sitting inside the house watching a football game when we heard this loud crash from outside. We lived a block from the fairgrounds and the carnival rides were being disassembled, so I just put it off as one of the rides or grandstands being torn down. Amy came down the steps yelling, "That was my car!" Sure enough, we ran outside and her car that had been parked along the road had been hit. Luckily, we were able to call the emergency responders to bring an ambulance for the driver of the other car and no one was seriously injured. Because of the minimum insurance requirements in Pennsylvania, we were now left with a damaged car and an underinsured motorist to cover the damage.

We ended up using our emergency fund for our deductible to get the car repaired until we could figure out payments with the insurance companies six months later. We rebuilt our emergency fund over the next few months and got back on track paying off debt.

The next item on our target list was student loans. I had been paying these for ten years since graduating and never knew anything different than the monthly payments. I was able to defer them while I was studying for my master's degree, so I still had two years left until they were paid off. Since we rolled the motorcycle and car payment into them, we were able to get rid of them within six months. This was really working! We were getting traction and we loved it!

About midway through the process, the burden of getting out from under this mess I created had become stressful. We were now paying off the last debt; which was the full size truck I had bought just before starting the classes. It was the only monthly payment left, but from our projections, we had over a year to go until we were out from under it. Not bad for a four year loan, but I am the type of person that when I set a personal goal and can see the end, it cannot get done fast enough. I always have to find a way to accelerate the schedule, especially when Dave Ramsey is telling you to get "Gazelle Intense."

Once again, God and prayer reached into our hearts and called us to see Father Scott at my local church. The topic of discussion that night was stress. He talked about all I had been going through without talking directly to me. He had the group close our eyes and meditate with him. He kept saying, "breathe Jesus in, exhale your stress out" and to "leave it all on the alter." I broke down and wept in the middle of a bunch of people I knew, but I left the church feeling refreshed and renewed. From that point on I was determined to, as the great exemplar of Christian faith Corrie Ten Boom is quoted as saying; "Use prayer as a steering wheel, not a spare tire."

I decided to completely turn my life over to God's will. I continued my prayers of thanksgiving and gratitude for a great job, a beautiful wife and food and shelter for us both. But I also began to pray that I would be guided and welcomed into a new lifestyle, other than just spinning the wheel, in order to do his work during my time here on earth.

I decided that contentment meant fixing my paid-for project truck and driving it. It had some repairs that needed to be completed in order for it to be road-worthy, but I did not have the garage space or proper tools to complete it at the time. So I found a local mechanic to fix it for a reasonable price and paid cash.

Since Amy and I were reinvigorated about our future together, had a new zest for life and were communicating better, we started to look at other aspects of our life and where our future was headed.

It was true that the town we lived in received a sizable amount of snowfall every year. The people we met during our years of living there were some of the most genuine people you will ever meet, but we were both getting depressed from the constant gloomy skies and precipitation and we complained about it constantly.

That winter was one of the worst winters for weather in recent history. Since we were in the snow belt of the Allegheny Mountains, it seemed like it did not stop snowing for several months. Several years before, I had bought one of the largest snow blowers available, but the piles along the driveway were about six feet high and it could no longer blow the snow over the piles.

I specifically remember one trip to Amy's hometown that winter. I started the day wearing long sleeves, a coat, hat and gloves while scraping ice off the windshield. When I arrived in Amy's hometown, it was in the mid-sixties and I did not need anything more than the long sleeves.

We decided it was time to stop complaining and do something about it. Until now, we had never had the option to move because our house was in disrepair and our money was tied up in payments. Since we were not going to take out another loan, we decided to postpone paying all extra money on the truck, with "gazelle intensity" and complete the remaining details of renovations to our house as cash became available.

I had been traveling about fifty percent of the time with my job as a manager. The rest of the time was spent managing budgets and schedules, creating status reports and planning the next trip. Management at my company agreed that I could perform these duties while working from home.

Like the three Magi, we decided to take a leap of faith and follow the light that was guiding us from within. We listed the house on the market with a top notch local realtor. We had three showings scheduled in the first week, and almost unbelievably, we accepted an offer one week later. Keep in mind this was during a recession with a slow housing market. This was a major sign to me that there was a higher power at work to send us in a new direction with life.

We targeted our old college town near Amy's parents and we were able to cash flow the move including realtor fees, bank fees, moving expenses plus a twenty percent down payment on a townhouse.

We had been in our townhouse for a couple of months and the motorcycle rally in our old town was fast approaching, but I did not have a motorcycle. I was on business travel at a conference and stopped by the Harley Davidson dealership to test ride some motorcycles. This really got me itching for another motorcycle especially since there was a sale with zero percent financing. Like an addict, I began trying to rationalize how I could use my full size truck with payments as a trade and how paying zero interest was no different than saving up payments each month. I sent several texts to Amy and she replied that she was talking to "the old Doug." I remembered what I had learned over the past year, and since I was now a changed person and able to listen to her opinion, I decided to leave. As an inside joke to those who listen to *The Dave Ramsey Show*, on the way home I heard the song "Money" by Pink Floyd which brought a smile to my face. It was a very liberating feeling knowing that I passed up a good deal for the betterment of our financial situation.

A few months later, we were able to sell the full size truck and we became "debt free" except for our ten year mortgage which we plan to have paid off earlier than the life of the loan.

To celebrate our new found freedom, we saved up money and bought kayaks. In the evenings and on the weekends we would spend time on the nearby lake. Not only did we get to enjoy nature, we got a good workout in the process. It reminded me of that summer after college when I got the chance to enjoy the water. It was as if we had hit the reset button on life with an opportunity to begin anew.

I remember Amy saying to me one evening, "We have spent more time together this summer than any other summer when we had a motorcycle." This made me swell with pride realizing that we were both content and finally in the right place in life.

IV. The Future

I find it strange how everything comes full circle, and I truly believe that everything happens for a reason. In order for us to move to a new town, Amy had resigned from her position at the jewelry store and was not able to land the type of fulfilling job she was seeking that summer. She spent the summer getting situated in the townhouse.

Our relocation put us within a half hour drive to her parents' house. During the fall after our move, I vividly remember the morning Amy's dad was diagnosed with cancer. I was working in the home office and she frantically came in telling me she had to go to the hospital to be with her parents. I dropped everything and went to the hospital with her. Luckily, later on, we learned it was in the early stages and treatable, but I still feel that God had other plans for Amy than working for a paycheck. It was as if he had known for over a year that we would be needed here in this town and set us on the proper course long before we knew why. Because we were on more solid financial ground, she postponed the job search and was able to be there through the appointments and procedures to help her parents during this battle.

During our journey out of debt, I had been talking to several close friends about our experiences and it resonated with one close friend of the family in particular. Living in a big city on an average income, he had always felt under pressure to meet his obligations every month. After a night out on the town, rather than pay for a cab, he and I decided to walk several miles to my parents' house. We discussed finances the entire way. Being the engineer and good with numbers, I was able to put together a rough budget for him immediately and explain to him about how long his journey would be. He was excited and as soon as we were able, we sat down and put together a budget and plan. It has given me great satisfaction to watch him work his plan and start gaining traction and winning financially.

As I ventured through this yearlong journey, I learned that contentment can be found not in purchasing material goods, but in being there for others in need and helping others set and achieve goals. It turns out I may have inherited the family's teaching gene after all.

This gave me inspiration to begin a new journey with personal financial counseling. I do not intend to make fortunes for myself, nor make people extremely wealthy. My intention is to help people realize their dreams that may otherwise seem hopeless due to high levels of stress and anxiety because of money issues. By understanding others and putting them first, I am better able to examine myself and become more self-aware about my impact on the world. I am more able to be generous and fulfill the spirit that resides within me.

I look forward to the life that lies ahead. I once told my friend Alex, "I would never trade anything for the feeling of freedom of the road that I get from riding my motorcycle." I would like to retract that statement now because I am enjoying this freedom more than I would have ever imagined. If God wills it, I plan to own another motorcycle again someday, but in the meantime, I will enjoy these times being content with the way things are.

As I was writing and reviewing this book, I thought to myself, "So what? What will others take away from my experiences?"
People sometimes ask if you had to describe yourself in one word, what would it be? In this aspect, I guess it would have to be "inspirational." If you are a sophomore or junior in college thinking that the end is so far out of sight that you will never get there, know that I have been there and I encourage you to persevere. If you are single trying to make it in a big city and win financially or spiritually, know that I have seen it done and that you can do it too. Married couples, I encourage you to talk more openly about

your household finances and to get in agreement with your goals and spending. When you align your values and are working toward one common goal, this will open other communication within your marriage and you will remember why you married that special someone in the first place.

I hope my experiences shared in this book can provide some guidance and inspiration for you to live your life to the fullest, whatever that may mean.

I encourage everyone in this seemingly haphazard world to slow down and enjoy the life we have been given. Let God work in your life and do not burden yourself with unnecessary stress by trying to get ahead of his plan for you.

Psalm 37:5,7 tells us,

> *"Commit everything you do to the Lord. Trust him to help you do it, and he will. . . Rest in the Lord; wait patiently for him to act. Don't be envious of evil men who prosper."*

The Lord works in mysterious ways. Some may chalk it up to coincidence, but I believe he has a plan for all of us. Sometimes we just need to be still and let God move for a while. If we just open our eyes, ears and hearts and allow him to speak to us, a whole new world will unravel before us.

Bibliography:

Dave Ramsey's Financial Peace University. Ramsey. The Lampo Group, Inc. 2007. DVD.

The Seven Pillars of Catholic Spirituality. Kelly. Beacon Publishing. 2009. DVD

Zander, Rosamund Stone and Benjamin. *The Art of Possibility*. New York. Penguin Books. 2002.

Verses are taken from *The Living Bible* copyright 1971. Used by permission of Tyndale House Publishers, Inc., Wheaton, IL 60189. All rights reserved.